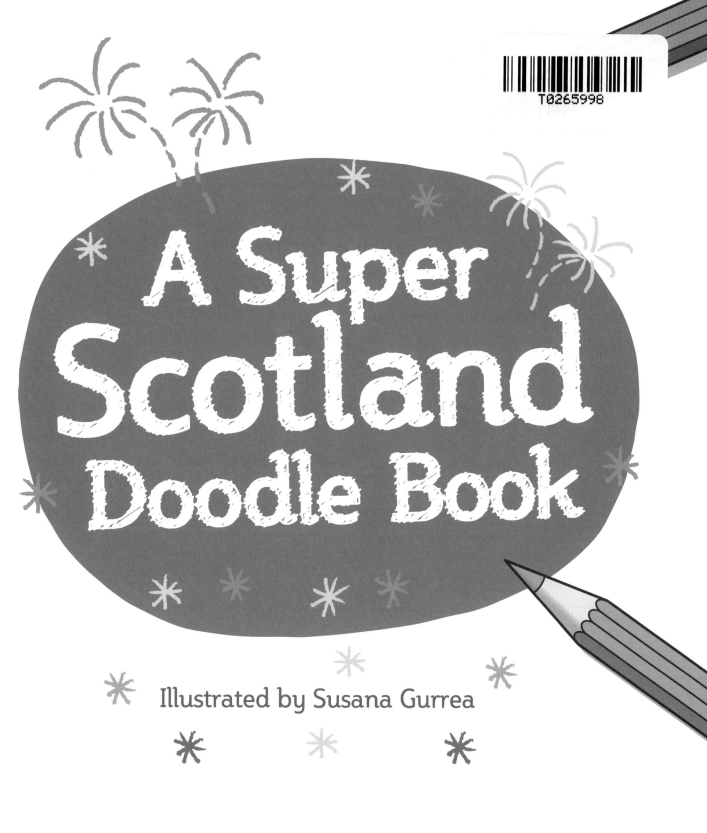

A Super Scotland Doodle Book

Illustrated by Susana Gurrea

Kelpies
World

Create a Scottish castle

Scotland is full of castles. Some of the most famous are Edinburgh Castle, Stirling Castle and Urquhart Castle at Loch Ness. Create your own castle and colour it in.

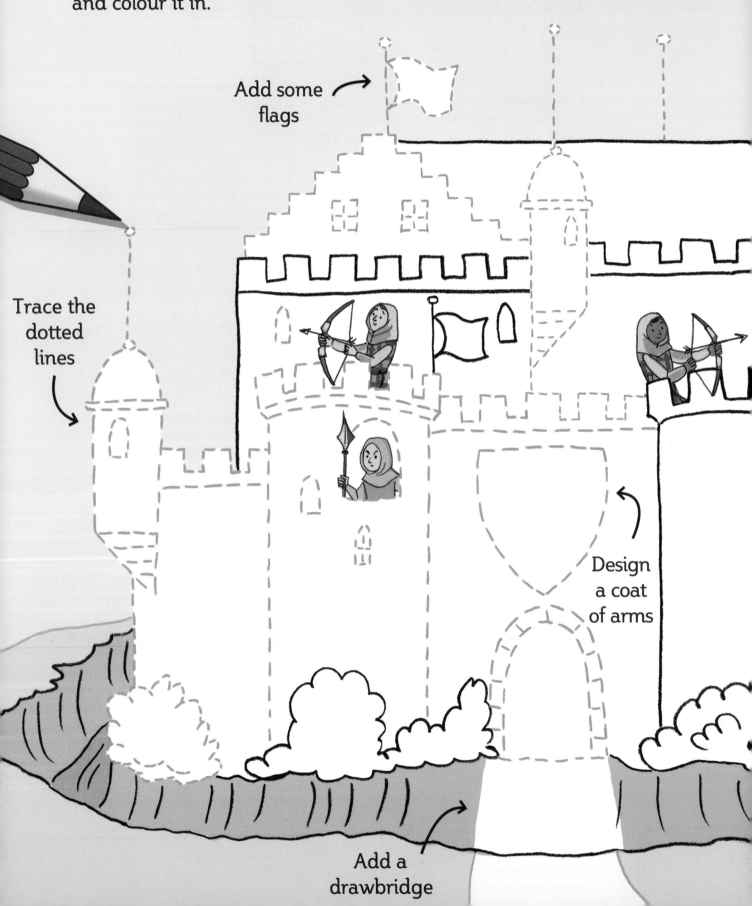

Add some flags

Trace the dotted lines

Design a coat of arms

Add a drawbridge

Colour in
the castle

Doodle some
visitors to the
castle

Colour the Glasgow crowd

The Duke of Wellington statue outside the Gallery of Modern Art in Glasgow always has a traffic cone on his head. Sometimes his horse has one too! Add hats to this Glasgow crowd.

Doodle hats

Colour in clothes

Why not try these hats?

Add a
lead for
the dog

Doodle patterns
on the dog's coat

Munro maze

Scotland has lots of high mountains called Munros. Help the Munro bagger climb to the top of Ben Nevis, the highest mountain in the UK.

Draw some clouds in the sky

Colour the skiers orange

Colour the hikers coming down red

START

Ben Nevis is taller than 300 double-decker buses on top of each other!

FINISH

Colour the hikers climbing up blue

Doodle Scottish monsters

Many people believe that the Loch Ness Monster (Nessie!) lives in Loch Ness, the deepest loch in Scotland. Doodle your own underwater monsters.

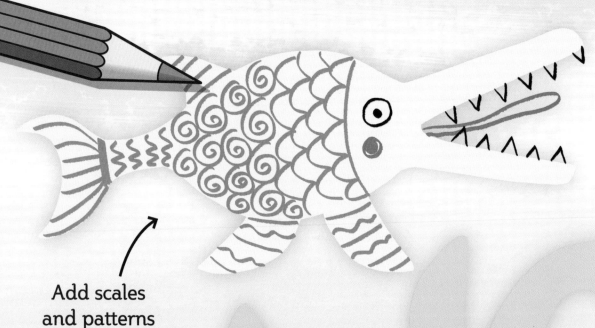

Add scales and patterns

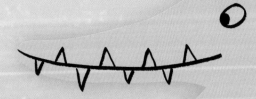

Loch Ness is so deep 140 cars stacked on top of each other wouldn't reach the bottom.

Draw your own monster here!

Which do you think is the real Nessie?

Colour the museum

Welcome to the main hall of the famous Kelvingrove Museum and Art Gallery in Glasgow. It is full of fascinating things, including a stuffed elephant! Colour in all the exhibits.

Sir Roger the elephant has been in the museum for over 100 years

Join the dots

Design the children's school uniforms

Doodle faces on the floating heads. Are they happy or sad?

Add faces and hair

Trace the giant spider crab

Design shields

Soldiers who fought in Scotland carried shields to defend themselves. Trace, colour or doodle designs on these shields.

Round shields called targes were carried by Scottish soldiers

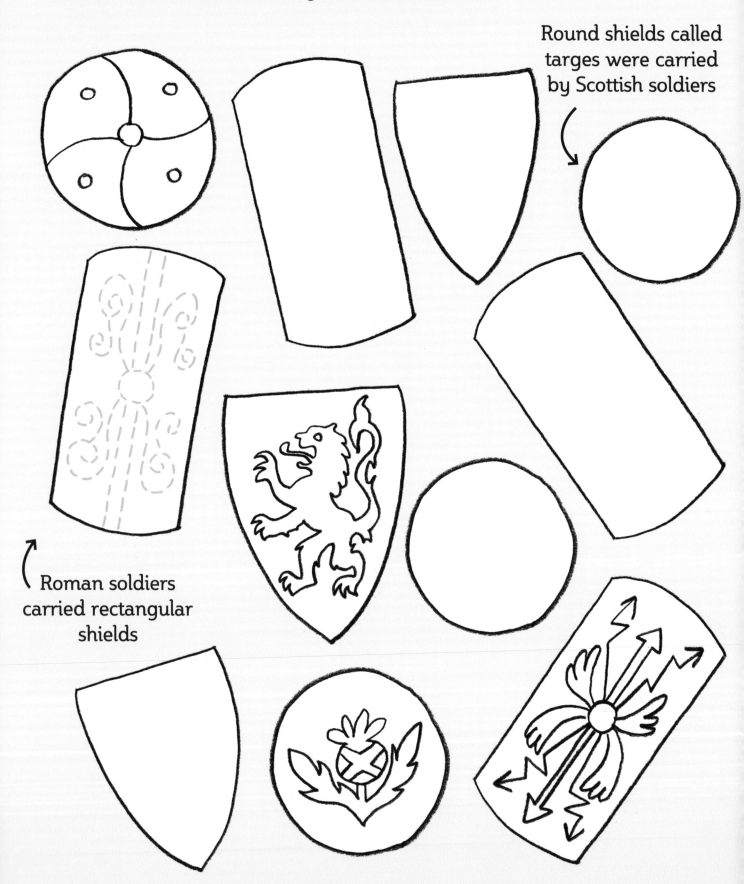

Roman soldiers carried rectangular shields

Vikings carried round wooden shields

Trace these designs

Trace Loch Lomond's wildlife

Visitors enjoy exploring the banks of Loch Lomond, between the lowlands and the Highlands of Scotland. Trace the plants and creatures reflected in the loch.

Doodle thistles and flowers

Red squirrels are very rare in the UK

Colour in the animals

The thistle is the national emblem of Scotland

Trace the reflections

Doodle the Edinburgh Tattoo audience

Thousands of people watch performers from around the world at the Royal Edinburgh Military Tattoo at Edinburgh Castle. Doodle the audience.

Add hair and hats

Colour and design clothes

Each night the Tattoo ends with a firework display. Draw some fireworks.

Oh, no, it's started to rain! Doodle some raindrops.

Draw faces

Design a Viking longboat

Vikings once lived in Scotland. Every year people in the Shetland Isles celebrate their Viking roots at the Up Helly Aa festival by setting a longboat on fire with burning torches. Design your own Viking longboat.

Doodle a pattern on the sail

Doodle a dragon head on the front of your longboat

Colour the torches

Design
Viking shields

Colour the North Coast 500

Travel all 516 miles of the North Coast 500 to see beautiful beaches and historic places. Colour the vehicles travelling along this famous route.

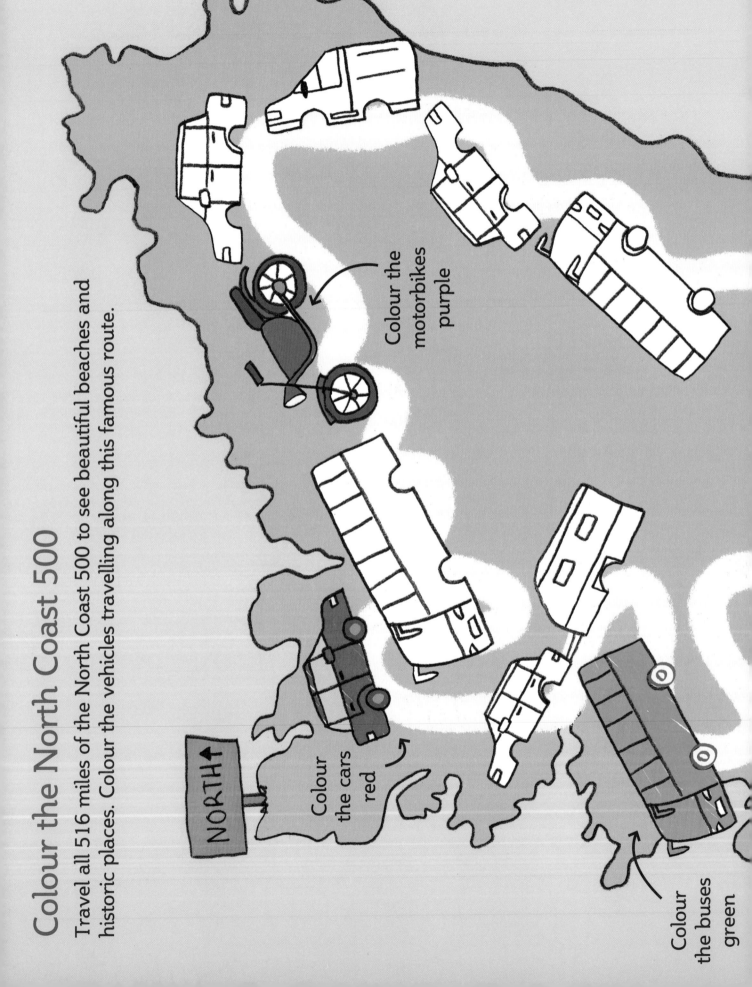

Colour the motorbikes purple

Colour the cars red

NORTH

Colour the buses green

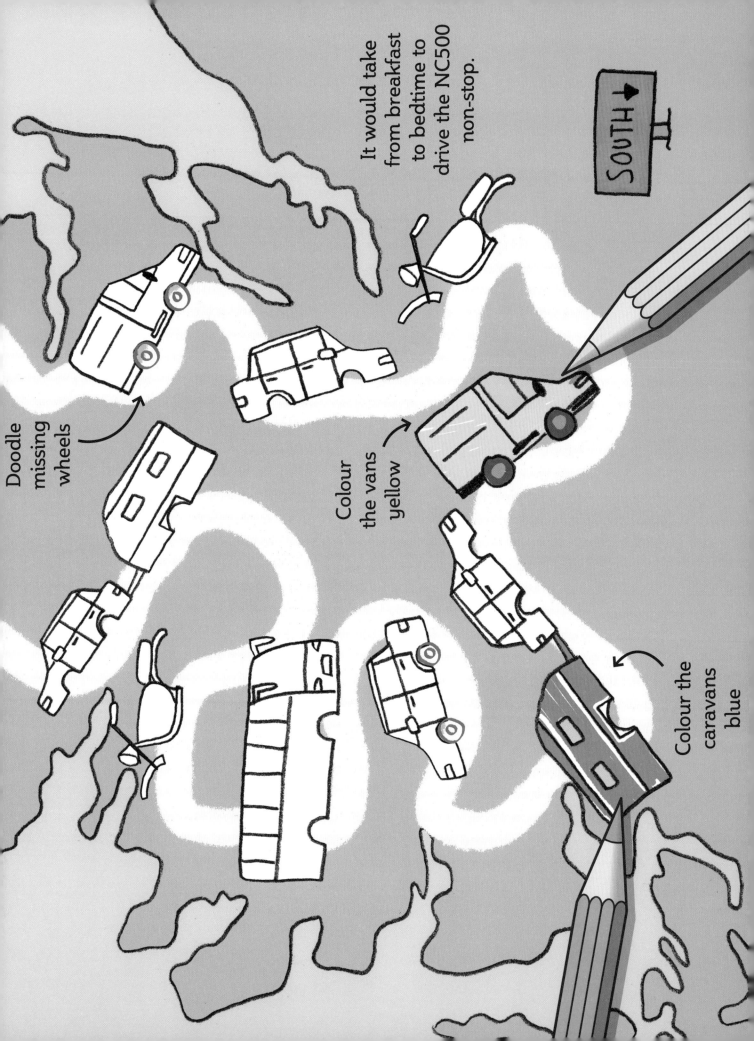

Doodle missing wheels

It would take from breakfast to bedtime to drive the NC500 non-stop.

SOUTH →

Colour the vans yellow

Colour the caravans blue

Colour the Isle of Skye

The waters around Skye are full of wonderful wildlife – even seals and dolphins! Colour the sea creatures and add more fish to the sea.

Add scales to the fish

Baby seals are called pups

Fill the sea with
colourful fish

Trace the
dotted animals

Design a railway

You can journey around Scotland by train to see the mountains, moors and lochs. Complete the track to take the train from Inverness to Edinburgh.

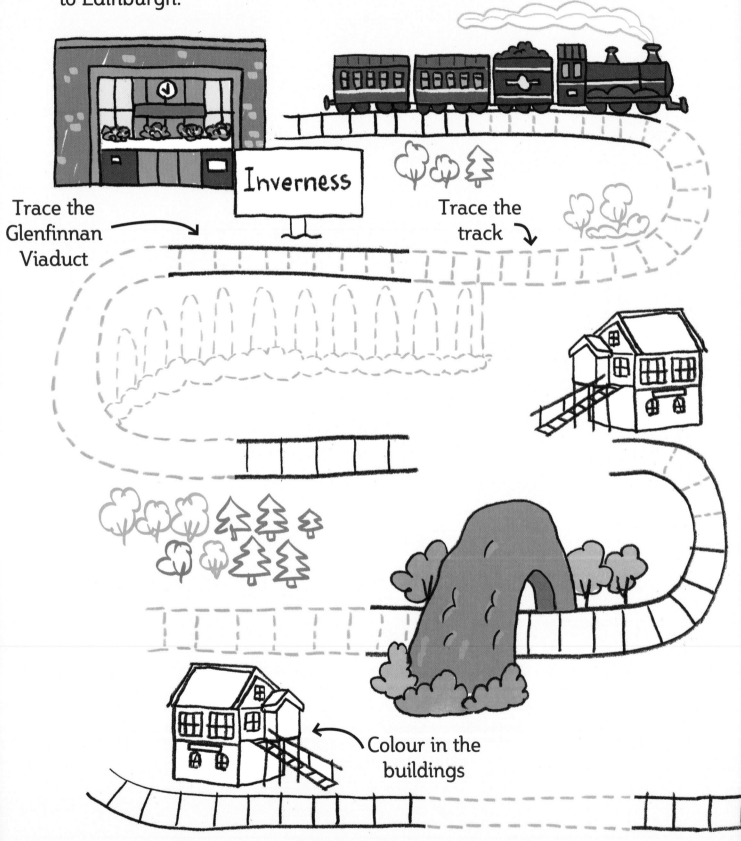

Inverness

Trace the Glenfinnan Viaduct

Trace the track

Colour in the buildings

The Forth Bridge is as long as 28 football pitches!

Trace the Forth Bridge

Doodle trees

Edinburgh Waverley

Colour a Stone Age village

Skara Brae, in the Orkney Islands, is a famous Neolithic village over 5,000 years old – and it can still be seen today. Colour the village as it might have looked long ago.

Colour the axes green

Colour the pots red

Skara Brae was buried in sand for thousands of years

Add smoke to the chimneys

Colour the fish blue

Add an exhibit

Welcome to V&A Dundee, Scotland's first design museum, where you can see pictures, objects and clothes. Add your own exhibits to the museum.

Colour the dress

Draw a statue

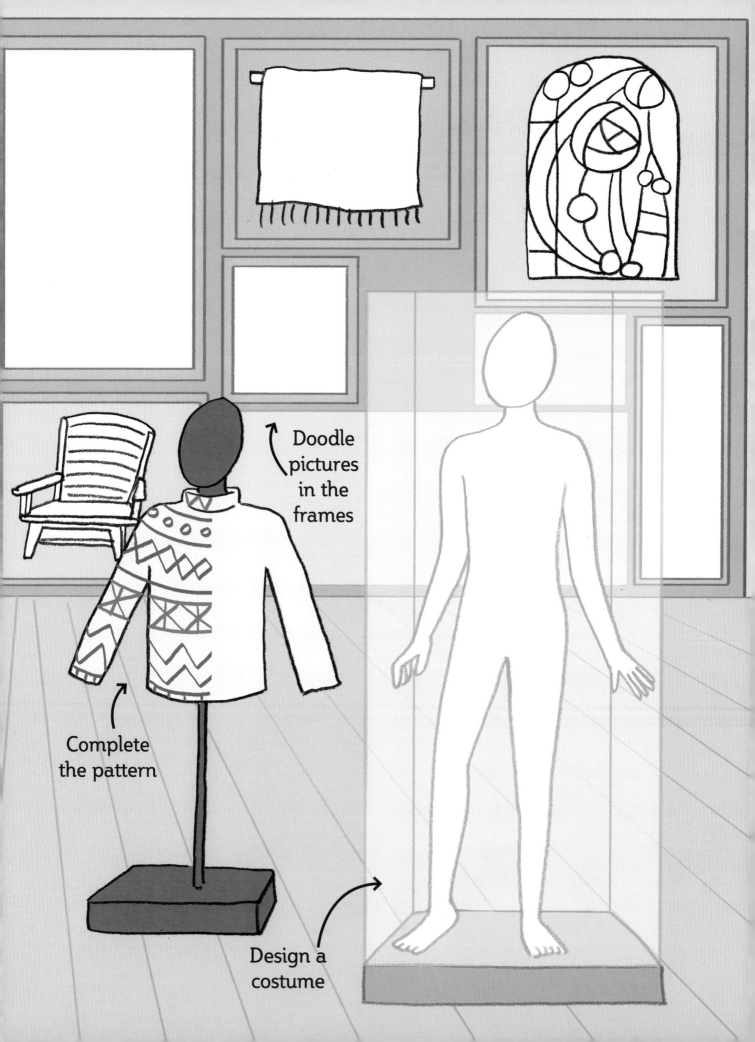

Doodle pictures in the frames

Complete the pattern

Design a costume

Follow the canal maze

Scotland has many canals, including the Union Canal, which is connected to the Forth & Clyde Canal by the famous Falkirk Wheel. Help the boat get to the Kelpies statues.

START

The Falkirk Wheel

Doodle flowers on the boats

Colour and add
patterns to the boats

The Kelpies statues are as tall as
10 elephants on top of each other!

FINISH

Doodle the Highland Games

Welcome to the Highland Games! They take place every summer all around Scotland. Come and meet farm animals and watch athletes tossing the caber and throwing hammers and weights.

Doodle wool on the sheep

Add hair to the Highland coos

Colour the competitors

Give the pigs tails and snouts

See inside a Scottish castle

Scottish castles were busy places where noble families lived, with servants who looked after them, and soldiers to guard them. Colour in the people who live in this castle.

Colour the soldiers brown

Colour the chairs yellow

Design your own shields

Doodle yourself here

Colour the servants green

Colour the royals blue

There have been over 2,000 castles in Scotland, although some are no longer standing

Create a tartan design

Scotland is famous for its tartans, and different clans, or families, each have their own patterns. Create your own tartans. What colour will you use?

Add red stripes to the green tartan

Design your own tartans

Add green stripes to the pink tartan

Doodle a tartan outfit for this Highland dancer

There are over 4,000 different tartan designs

Add blue stripes to the yellow tartan

Doodle the fireworks

Edinburgh, Scotland's capital city, is famous for its Hogmanay fireworks display on New Year's Eve. Doodle your own fireworks and colour Edinburgh's famous landmarks.

Arthur's Seat

Edinburgh Castle

Balmoral Hotel

Scott Monument

Dugald Stewart Monument

Send a postcard

Doodle your favourite scene from Scotland on this postcard.

Have loads more fun with

join the dots

look and find

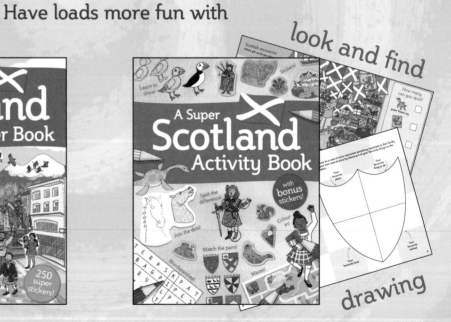

stickers

drawing

To my family with love – S.G.

Kelpies is an imprint of Floris Books. First published in 2019 by Floris Books. Second printing 2023. Illustrations © 2019 Susana Gurrea
Susana Gurrea asserts her right under the Copyright, Designs and Patents Act 1988 to be recognised as the Illustrator of this Work
All rights reserved. No part of this book may be reproduced without prior permission of Floris Books, Edinburgh www.florisbooks.co.uk
British Library CIP Data available ISBN 978-178250-557-0 Printed in China by Leo Paper Products Ltd

MIX
Paper | Supporting
responsible forestry
FSC® C020056

Floris Books supports sustainable forest
management by printing this book on
Forest Stewardship Council® certified paper